W9-CRX-603

CH

CELEBRATING KWANZAA

BY BARBARA M. LINDE

Gareth Stevens
PUBLISHING

Please visit our website, www.garethstevens.com. For a free color catalog of all our high-quality books, call toll free 1-800-542-2595 or fax 1-877-542-2596.

Library of Congress Cataloging-in-Publication Data

Names: Linde, Barbara M., author.
Title: Celebrating Kwanzaa / Barbara M. Linde.
Description: New York : Gareth Stevens Publishing, 2020.
| Series: The history of our holidays | Includes index.
Identifiers: LCCN 2018055438| ISBN 9781538238783 (pbk.)
| ISBN 9781538238806 (library bound) | ISBN 9781538238790 (6 pack)
Subjects: LCSH: Kwanzaa–Juvenile literature.
| African Americans–Social life and customs–Juvenile literature.
Classification: LCC GT4403 .L56 2020 | DDC 394.2612–dc23
LC record available at https://lccn.loc.gov/2018055438

Published in 2020 by
Gareth Stevens Publishing
111 East 14th Street, Suite 349
New York, NY 10003

Copyright © 2020 Gareth Stevens Publishing

Designer: Laura Bowen
Editor: Barbara Linde

Photo credits: Cover, p. 1 Ailisa/Shutterstock.com; pp. 2–24 (background texture) secondcorner/Shutterstock.com; pp. 3–24 (background flags) saicle/Shutterstock.com; pp. 5 (top), 13 SAUL LOEB/AFP/Getty Images; p. 5 (bottom) Shahar Azran/WireImage/Getty Images; p. 7 Bettmann/Bettmann/Getty Images; p. 11 Portland Press Herald/Portland Press Herald/Getty Images; p. 15 Connie Coleman/Photographer's Choice/Getty Images; p. 17 Inti St. Clair/Photodisc/Getty Images; p. 19 Miami Herald/Tribune News Service/Getty Images; p. 21 Hill Street Studios LLC/DigitalVision/Getty Images.

Printed in the United States of America

CPSIA compliance information: Batch #CS19GS: For further information contact Gareth Stevens, New York, New York at 1-800-542-2595

CONTENTS

Boldface words appear in the glossary.

A Happy Celebration

This happy **celebration** has drums and dances. It has songs, stories, and games. It's 7 days long. There's a candle for each night. There are gifts. Families eat tasty food and use a special cup. Let's learn all about the holiday called Kwanzaa (KWAN-za)!

The Reason for the Holiday

Dr. Maulana Karenga started Kwanzaa in 1966. He wanted to help African Americans honor their African **ancestors**. He chose December 26 to January 1 for the holiday. Many African groups gather their crops around that time. The name *Kwanzaa* comes from the phrase *matunda ya kwanza,* or "first fruits of the **harvest**."

Dr. Karenga, 1966

The Seven Principles

Seven **principles** are celebrated during Kwanzaa. The word *Kwanzaa* has seven letters—one for each principle! These ideas help African Americans learn about their ancestors and their values. They show people how to live good lives. People talk about one principle each day.

THE SEVEN PRINCIPLES

Here are the seven principles and their names in English and Swahili, an African language.

DECEMBER

26th	unity	*umoja* (oo-MO-jah)
27th	self-determination	*kujichagulia* (koo-jee-cha-GOO-lee-yah)
28th	work	*ujima* (oo-JEE-mah)
29th	business	*ujamaa* (oo-jah-MAH-ah)
30th	purpose	*nia* (NEE-ah)
31st	creativity	*kuumba* (koo-OOM-bah)

JANUARY

| 1st | faith | *imani* (ee-MAH-nee) |

Every day someone asks, "*Habari gani (ha-bar-ri-ga-ni)?*" or "What's the news?" Then they talk about the day's principle. Unity is about belonging to a family and a **race**. Self-determination means learning how to be yourself. Work is helping each other.

KWANZAA,
NGUZO SABA
The Seven Principles of KWANZAA:

...A__ (unity) __ to strive for and maintain unity in the family,
community, nation and race

KUJICHAGULIA __ (self-determination) __ to define, name, created for and speak for ourselves instead of being defined, named,
created for and spoken for by others

UJIMA __ (collective work and responsibility) __ to build and
maintain our community together, and to make our sister's and
brother's problems our problems and to solve them together

UJAMAA __ (cooperative economics) __ to build and maintain our
own stores, shops, and other businesses, and to profit together

NIA __ (purpose) __ to make our collective vocation the building
and development of our community, in order to restore our people
to their traditional greatness

KUUMBA __ (creativity) __ to do always as much as we can, in the
way we can, in order to leave our community more beautiful than
beneficial than we inherited it

IMANI __ (faith) __ to believe with all our hearts in our people, our
parents, our teachers and our leaders and the righteousness and victory
of our struggle

Maulana Karenga

11

Business is about having community stores and shopping in them. Purpose is about honoring **traditions**. Creativity is about doing things for the good of the community, such as making beautiful Kwanzaa decorations. Faith is about believing in the African American community.

The Seven Symbols

During Kwanzaa, a straw mat meaning tradition is put down, and six symbols go on it. The unity cup is for family. The crops are for the harvest. An ear of corn is set out for each child. Gifts symbolize the principles. Candles and a candleholder are set down, too.

15

A Candle Each Night

Each candle is a symbol for one principle. The black candle is a symbol for unity. It's lit on the first night. Then red and green candles are lit on the other nights. The candleholder, or *kinara*, is a symbol for the African ancestors.

A Big Feast

On December 31, many families have a big Kwanzaa feast called the *karamu*. Some people wear African-style clothes. Everyone sips from the unity cup. They eat sweet potatoes, bananas, and other tasty foods. There's dancing, singing, and drumming.

A Day to Think

The parties and games are all done by January 1. On that day people quietly think about their ancestors and their community. They plan how they want to live in the new year. Friends and families often give gifts to help them remember the principles.

GLOSSARY

ancestor: a family member who lived long before you

celebration: a time to show happiness for an event through activities such as eating or playing music

harvest: crops brought in at the end of a growing season

principle: a belief or truth

race: a group of people that have features, such as skin and hair, that look alike

tradition: a long-practiced custom

FOR MORE INFORMATION

BOOKS

Minnick-Taylor, Kathleen. *Kwanzaa: How to Celebrate It in Your Home.* Madison, WI: Praxis Publications Incorporated, 2013.

Otto, Carolyn B. *Holidays Around the World: Celebrate Kwanzaa.* Washington, DC: National Geographic Children's Books, 2017.

WEBSITES

Activity Village.co.uk: Kwanzaa
www.activityvillage.co.uk/kwanzaa
Learn the history of the Kwanzaa holiday. Get instructions on making traditional Kwanzaa crafts and download coloring cards and pages.

The Official Kwanzaa Website
www.officialkwanzaawebsite.org/index.shtml
Find out how and why Dr. Maulana Karenga founded Kwanzaa. Learn how to celebrate the holiday.

INDEX